The Tribe of the Thin Ankles

Surviving, Striving and Thriving with
Charcot-Marie-Tooth Disease

By Clark Semmes

DEDICATION

This book is for Marcia, my inspiration, my muse, my partner-in-crime, my co-worker, and my best friend. You are the reason for everything I do. Aimer, ce n'est pas se regarder l'un l'autre, c'est regarder ensemble dans la même direction.

This book is also for the board, staff, and members of the CMTA and for everyone in the world who has Charcot-Marie-Tooth disease. Thank you to all the folks out there who have CMT, but don't let CMT have them. Thank you to everyone who feels the bite, but moves forward regardless. Thank you to everyone who has neuropathy and muscle ache and nerve pain and muscle loss, but who also has dreams and goals and aspirations. Thank you to everyone who pushes through the pain in pursuit of the sublime. We are all members of the same tribe, united in our curious affliction, and working together we will one day find a cure! On that glorious day, CMT will join smallpox, polio, rubella, mumps, malaria, and a host of other diseases that once plagued mankind and are now largely or completely eradicated. Do not wait for others to act. The challenge is our own. Our fates reside in our own determination.

Thank you to Robert Carter for letting me use his illustration of the unraveling foot from the June 9, 2015 Washington Post article about CMT. For more of Robert's amazing art work please visit www.crackedhat.com.

Most importantly, thank you to everyone who took the time to tell me their stories. Thank you to Steve O'Donnell, Chelsea Singer, James Cuizon, Anthony Zahn, Tau and Eoin O'Sullivan, Jim Moneyhon, Aron Taylor, Vicki Halfyard, Jeana Sweeny, Jonah Berger, Bethany Meloche, Brittany Wright, Shawna Feely, Elizabeth Ouellette and Patrick Livney. Your stories inspired me and I hope they inspire others as well.

CONTENTS

1

The Tribe

"Find Your Tribe. You know, the ones that make you feel the most YOU. The ones that lift you up and help you remember who you really are. The ones that remind you that a blip in the road is just that, a blip. "

Jennifer Pastiloff

The Tribe

Charcot-Marie-Tooth disease is a degenerative neuromuscular disorder that affects one in 2,500 people around the world, yet somehow remains largely unknown. Charcot-Marie-Tooth, or simply CMT, causes a slow deterioration in the nerves that carry signals from our brains to our muscles. Those of us who have the disease feel it most acutely in the places where our nerves must make their longest journey, most notably in our feet and in our hands. As the nerves to our hands and feet deteriorate, the muscles in these locations atrophy. This leads to many problems, the most visible of which is a distinct thinning of the ankles.

While those of us who have this disease are widely dispersed, the Internet and social media have allowed us to find one another, come together, and organize. We have shifted from a wide and dispersed collection of individuals into a unified group with an organization that represents us, a scientific research agenda and a growing sense of community. We are no longer a far-flung group of unconnected individuals. We are a tribe.

Some refer to our tribe as CMTers, but I find the designation undescriptive. Some call us CMT patients, but patience is something we lack. I prefer a name that refers to our most distinguishing feature and the manner in which we frequently identify one another. We are the Tribe of the Thin Ankles.

What About Your Teeth?

One of the problems is the name - Charcot-Marie-Tooth. It is just not a name that fastens itself in the minds of most Americans - too long, too French, too many hyphens. No one can remember it. Most of us who have it just call it CMT. Lots of my friends call it "that Shark Tooth thing."

It is ironic, because Jean-Martin Charcot was a superstar of his era. In his time he was one of the most famous doctors in the world. People from all over the world, including many Americans, traveled to Paris just to hear his lectures. In his day, Charcot's name would have rung a bell in the minds of educated people all over the world. He was the French doctor who was bringing neurology out of the dark ages. He was the man who was explaining why peculiar maladies inhibited the ability of some people to walk normally or make their hands obey their will. A disease whose name started with Charcot would have been recognized as a neurologic malady named, in part, after the most famous neurologist in the world. But Jean-Martin Charcot's era was the late 1800s. Today his name is largely forgotten, certainly by most Americans, and Charcot-Marie-Tooth is just a strange name for a little known disease.

Lou Gehrig's Disease- there is a handle that Americans can remember. It is short, it is simple, it is self-explanatory. Lou Gehrig's disease is the disease that killed Lou Gehrig, the famous American ball player. It is simple, easy to remember. That's what you want in a disease name. That's what you want when raising awareness for an insidious neurologic condition. Perhaps one day a really famous American will get CMT, and we will rename our disease. Justin Bieber Disease – that would work. Donald Trump Disease – people would remember that name! I am not wishing any ill will on Justin Bieber or Donald Trump. I'm just saying. At least people would recognize the name.

A Disease That Affects Sharks?

Another problem with Charcot-Marie-Tooth Disease is that it isn't normally fatal. Cancer, heart disease, multiple sclerosis, Lou Gehrig's Disease; all these diseases can kill you. Fatal diseases tend to get the big funding. CMT is, for the most part, non-fatal. Don't get me wrong, it can curl your hands and feet and drive you crazy, but because it is non-fatal it gets less attention than other diseases. Perhaps that is another reason it is largely unknown.

There are other problems. Charcot-Marie-Tooth is frequently misdiagnosed or missed altogether. Many people who have it don't know they have it. Lots of things can cause neuropathy, including diabetes, which is rampant in this country. Confirming CMT requires an elaborate nerve conduction study. Diagnosing a CMT subtype requires genetic testing, which, until recently, was an expensive and time-consuming proposition.

Finally, some of us who have CMT hide our disease. Why? Fear getting fired from our jobs is one cause. This was a real possibility in the not-too-distant past, and something that still happens today despite the fact that it is illegal. Maybe we're worried that a diagnosis early in life will preclude getting health insurance later on. Prior to the Affordable Care Act (Obamacare), this was a real possibility.

For all these reasons, Charcot-Marie-Tooth is the most common disease that no one has heard of. CMT affects one in 2,500 people, and some doctors believe this number is wildly understated.

CMT Types and Subtypes

There are five main types of CMT, conveniently designated as Type 1, Type 2, Type 3, Type 4, and Type X. CMT Type 1 causes a deterioration of the sheath around the nerves, which is called the myelin sheath. Most people use the analogy of the plastic coating that surrounds an electrical cord. CMT Type 2 causes a deterioration of the nerve itself - the metal wire inside the plastic coating.

In order to help make a definitive diagnosis of CMT, and to provide some indication of the type, a neurologist will do a test called a Nerve Conduction Study. Basically, they wheel in a little machine with lots of wires and then hook up a bunch of little sensor pads to various parts of your feet or fingers. Then, they take an electrically charged wand, and they touch it to your elbow or your knee, or some other part of your body close to where the nerves to your extremities are located. The test is repeated at different electrical strengths. What the person receiving the tests feels is an electric jolt. What you want to see is your fingers or your toes suddenly jumping when the electrical charge hits them.

The purpose of the test is to measure the speed and the strength of the electrical signal as it travels down the nerves of your arms or legs. A slow or weakened electrical signal is a strong indication of CMT. The relative speed and strength of the electrical signal indicates whether the problem resides in the nerve or the sheath surrounding it, and the neurologist may make a determination as to whether it is Type 1 or Type 2.

I've never heard anyone with CMT say anything particularly nice about undergoing a nerve conduction study. To me, it's like being repeatedly touched by a weak cattle prod. It's also very odd to watch your fingers and toes suddenly jump as a jolt of electricity hits them. But in reality, it is far better if your digits give a healthy jump, which means that the electrical signal has reached its destination. I remember watching my big toe during my first nerve conduction study. Regardless of the strength of the electrical pulse coursing down my leg, my big toe never gave the slightest twitch. It was not a good sign.

CMT types are further broken down into numerous subtypes. The subtypes are determined by the exact gene where a problematic mutation is located. I work on computers for a living, so I use the analogy of software code. Software code frequently has coding errors, sometimes referred to as bugs. If a program has bugs, it will not work correctly. To me, genetic mutations are like software coding errors. Some bugs are simple and easy to identify. Maybe the person who wrote the code put a comma instead of a period on one particular line of code. This might be common and a relatively simple bug. Other bugs could be more complicated.

CMT Type 1A is an example of a common and relatively simple genetic mutation. Approximately 50 percent of people with CMT have CMT1A. As I write this, the number of identified genetic mutations is somewhere in the 80s. More are being identified all the time. There are three additional types of CMT, CMT Type 3, CMT Type 4, and CMT Type X. For more information, visit the CMTA website at www.cmtausa.org.

Determining a person's CMT subtype is done through genetic testing. Unlike the nerve conduction study, genetic testing is painless. Thanks to recent advances in genetics, the cost of genetic testing has also dropped dramatically. Since there is no currently no cure for CMT, some people choose to forego genetic testing to determine their CMT subtype. But for those who are interested in participating in clinical trials once a drug treatment is ready, a CMT subtype diagnosis will be a requirement.

2

Who Were Charcot, Marie and Tooth?

"What is past is prologue"

W. Shakespeare

The names Charcot, Marie, and Tooth are all too familiar. But what do we know about the men behind the surnames—Jean-Martín Charcot, Pierre Marie and Henry Howard Tooth?

Now widely considered the father of modern neurology, Jean-Martín Charcot was a rock star of French medicine in his day. Born to a middle-class family in Paris in 1825, Charcot showed an early interest in art. He was torn between a career as an artist and one as a physician, but in the end decided on medicine. Some biographers believe that Charcot's powers of observation and visual documentation, honed as an artist, helped him identify and document previously uncategorized medical conditions.

Charcot did well in school and was soon working at the famous Salpetriere Hospital in Paris (named for the original use of the site as a storage depot for saltpeter, which is used in making gunpowder). He thrived there and in time was the first to describe at least 15 neurological conditions now named after him, including:

- Charcot's disease (also known as ALS or Lou Gehrig's disease)
- Charcot's joint
- Charcot's artery
- Charcot–Wilbrand Syndrome
- Charcot's triad of MS
- And, of course, Charcot-Marie-Tooth disease.

Charcot's weekly lectures at the hospital were a hot ticket, drawing students from all over Europe and the United States. Some of Charcot's students went on to garner great fame, including Sigmund Freud, Pierre Marie, and Georges Gilles de la Tourette.

While his contributions to the study of the human nervous system are undeniable, Charcot's forays into psychology were not as fruitful. Charcot initially believed that "hysteria" was a neurological disorder that only affected young women. However, by the end of his life, he had concluded that hysteria was psychological in origin and affected both sexes. Charcot passed away on August 16, 1893, at the age of 67. He was survived by two sons, one of whom became a doctor and a polar explorer. Charcot Island in Antarctica was discovered by Jean Baptiste Charcot and was named for his father.

While not as well-known as Charcot, Pierre Marie was a brilliant physician who made many important contributions to the field of neurology. Early in his career, Marie was working as an assistant to Charcot when they became interested in a group of patients with similarly misshapen feet and thin ankles. Their research resulted in an 1886 paper in the Revue Medicale about a unique form of progressive muscular atrophy that would later be called Charcot-Marie-Tooth disease. Like Charcot, Marie published extensively, and numerous diseases and syndromes bear his name. He also became the first General Secretary of the French Neurology Society and co-founder of the Neurologic Review.

Howard Henry Tooth was the odd man out. Unlike Charcot and Marie, who were French, Tooth was an Englishman. In pursuit of his medical degree, Tooth wrote a 43-page dissertation entitled "The Peroneal Type of Progressive Muscular Atrophy." Like the paper by Charcot and Marie, Tooth's dissertation described the common features of what is now known as Charcot-Marie-Tooth disease. Tooth went on to have a respectable career as a physician and an officer in the British military, but he wrote no further papers of note and had no other diseases named after him. He served honorably in the Boer War in South Africa, was married twice and died at his home at Hadleigh, Suffolk, at the advanced age of 86.

Unfortunately, while Charcot, Marie, and Tooth provided the first detailed description of CMT, they didn't cure it. That challenge belongs to the current generation of doctors and scientists. With the technology and knowledge now available, and with the support of the entire CMT community, the next step is stopping and reversing the damages that CMT inflicts.

3

The Survivors

"To live is to suffer,
To survive is to find some meaning in the suffering"

Friedrich Nietzsche

Bob Williams & Steve O'Donnell

When I was depressed following my diagnosis with CMT, a good friend told me about a guy in my neighborhood who had CMT and swam across the Chesapeake Bay every year to raise funds to for CMT research. His name was Steve O'Donnell. I decided I had to meet this guy, got his phone number, and gave him a call. He immediately invited me over to his house. Despite a serious case of CMT, Steve is a successful businessman, an amazing athlete, and a devoted husband and father. Once I met Steve, I quickly decided I could no longer feel sorry for myself. Here is his story:

Steve O'Donnell

Steve watched from the clouds as the paramedics cut his favorite golf pants from his body. He remembers saying to himself: "Wait. It's not time for me to check out. I have two kids to raise." The person in the white robe floating next to him faded into the clouds and he woke up later that evening in the Shock Trauma Unit at the University of Maryland, the survivor of a near-fatal car accident.

He was unaware of his surroundings, and tied down to the bed for fear he had broken his neck. Two MRIs revealed that it was not. Released the next day to the care of his mother-in-law, an ICU nurse, Steve's journey to recovery was just beginning. Sleeping and hospital visits took up most of his time. A few weeks after the accident, Steve realized he was in trouble when he was unable to complete the small task of grocery shopping. Steve searched for the "A" team of doctors. He found his savior in Dr. Janine Goode, who immediately put him on a strict regimen of limited work and lots of sleep.

Dr. Goode limited Steve to working one hour a day for the first month, then two hours a day for the next and so on until he was able to get back to work full time. Dr. Goode also ordered Steve to take a nap every day at the same time and to get eight to ten hours of uninterrupted sleep each night – difficult with a 6-week-old baby and toddler at home "You need to heal your brain and the way you do that is by rest," she said. Steve followed the instructions to the letter and was released after eight months in Dr. Goode's care.

Soon after, Steve was watching "The Lion King " with his daughter Jaime. When the ghost of Simba's father told the young lion, "You are more than you have become," the words went straight through Steve. He got up off the coach and drove 250 miles to quit his job and try his luck at "pitching" in business.

Today, Steve is a highly successful businessman with his own multimillion dollar steel company. Diagnosed years ago with CMT, Steve accepted the challenge of his illness by joining the board of the CMTA (he is the longest serving board member) and tirelessly raising money for the organization. Steve is also an amazing athlete. For many years, Steve's yearly fundraiser was a swim across the Chesapeake Bay he called "Swim for the Cure." Today the Swim for the Cure has morphed into The Oxford Biathlon, and Steve leads a team of athletes in a one-mile swim followed by a 20-mile bike ride. Over the years, Steve's swim has raised well over a million dollars for the CMTA.

Following his example, Steve's children are also excelling. Steve's daughter Jaime spent the summer of 2015 interning at Goldman Sachs, and was recently hired as a full-time employee. Steve's son Sean represented Maryland in the lifeguard Olympics. Whatever path they choose, Jaime and Sean can't help but be inspired by their old man, and the way he has taken the lemons of life and turned them into lemonade.

Chelsea Singer

I first became aware of Chelsea Singer when she posted an incredible picture of herself in a seemingly impossible yoga pose on a beach. I shared the post, she e-mailed me, and we were soon in contact. What inspires me most about Chelsea is her relentlessly positive attitude in the face of adversity. Since this article was printed, Chelsea has received numerous requests for her yoga DVDs and founded an organization called CMTYOGA. Here is her story:

Chelsea Singer

Growing up in Michigan, Chelsea Singer did not realize her feet were misshapen. She thought she was just growing faster than everyone else. She wasn't diagnosed until the age of 11, when her mother underwent foot surgery for her own CMT. Chelsea's struggles with CMT were compounded by watching her mother succumb to a pain pill addiction, and she left Michigan at the age of 15 for a new life in Colorado.

While still in her teens, Chelsea opted for surgery to ensure she would not end up in chronic pain like her mother. Chelsea planned to have surgery on her left foot first, then her right. The surgery included straightening her toes, correcting her bunions, having a screw inserted into her ankle and cutting her heel cords. Despite the fact that cutting the heel cord was the only really successful aspect of the first surgery, after three months of recovery she felt physically and mentally strong enough to have the same procedures done on her right foot.

While the surgery on her left foot was not a complete success, the surgery on her right foot was a downright disaster. Chelsea recalls screaming in pain as the doctor unwrapped her bandages at her post-surgery appointment. Everything from her right knee down was black. Four emergency surgeries followed, and Chelsea twice almost had her right foot amputated. Finally a long hospital stay and the application of leeches on her toes (a new leech every 45 minutes for an entire week) brought circulation back to Chelsea's toes and she managed to keep both her feet, but the experience left her mentally scarred and physically weakened. At the time of her discharge, she was unable to stand on her left leg for more than a few seconds at a time.

Bedbound for almost three months, Chelsea grew depressed and nearly suicidal. When she finally regained her strength, she resolved to leave the cold behind forever and moved to St. Petersburg, Florida. While she was able to leave the weather behind, she could not do the same with her own physical and emotional trauma. Hospitals and even medical commercials filled her with anxiety. Eventually she was diagnosed with post-traumatic stress disorder (PTSD) and began getting counseling.

Chelsea reluctantly tried her first-ever yoga class at the age of 26. While she initially thought there was no way she could handle the physical challenge, Chelsea quickly discovered she loved yoga. Within a year, she was in a teacher training program and is now a nationally certified instructor.

Chelsea's yoga practice focuses on the meditative aspects of yoga, including visualizing energy, breathing and healing energy. She teaches many classes, including a free one sponsored by the Muscular Dystrophy Association, and finds it a blessing to do something she loves that is also good for her. Today Chelsea meets lots of people with CMT and has even made DVDs for people who cannot attend her class in St. Petersburg.

One of the things that Chelsea loves most is teaching others not to be ashamed of their disability. She remembers when she was unwilling to let anyone see her bare feet, and now she's barefoot most of the day. Chelsea looks forward to reaching an even larger audience with her message of yoga's healing powers. She has formed an informal support group with her friends Tia and Elisa that they call the CMT Sisterhood. They meet once a month and the group has now grown to seven.

Namaste, Chelsea and the CMT Sisterhood!

Yoga and CMT

By Chelsea Singer

When most people hear the word yoga they think only of a physical exercise. True yoga has actually nothing to do with physical movement: It is an inner practice rather than an outer one. Yoga is a practice of self love, of letting go and of surrender.

While the physical practice of yoga can greatly benefit and enhance the quality of life for people living with CMT, it is not the only form of yoga. If physical poses cannot be a part of where you are in your life right now, you can still greatly benefit from yoga. Yoga means union of the soul with spirit. True yoga, as practiced in India for thousands of years, is meditation.

During yoga classes with people who have all different forms of CMT, the main focus is on deep breathing and visualization. If someone cannot do a physical pose, they can close their eyes, send a deep breath to the body part, and visualize themselves doing the pose. The mind is a powerful tool. And when our bodies do not work the way we wish they did, we can use our mind and will power to aid in healing on all levels - physical, mental and spiritual.

Yoga is a universal practice that can benefit anyone, no matter their age or physical ability. It doesn't matter if you are in a wheelchair, use an oxygen machine or are paralyzed. Even if we cannot do physical poses, we can all benefit from stilling our restless minds. That is what we try to achieve in yoga meditation in order to experience a joy, a bliss, a love and a peace that is beyond our limited human comprehension.

Unless you live on a beautiful tropical island with gorgeous weather year round, it's unrealistic to think you will have the ideal surroundings for your yoga practice. If you do practice yoga at home - whether it's a yoga DVD with physical movements or a guided meditation - turn your area into a sacred space. Make your practice something you look forward too rather than dread. Dim your lights and play some relaxing music. You can light candles, use an oil burner or burn incense to help relax.

If an at-home practice is not for you and you want to try a class, that's wonderful too! But make sure you know in advance as much about the class style, teacher and space to make sure it's right for you. Call around and talk in detail to the owner or teacher about the class and any limitations you may have. It's important that you both call ahead of time and go up to the teacher before the class starts. Yoga teachers see a lot of students. The best way to ensure the instructor knows you have limitations is to approach them right before a class starts. That way they can guide you as to what poses you should or shouldn't do.

Going into a class can be super nerve-racking, especially knowing ahead of time you'll probably face different challenges than other students. The first step is starting.

Go in with an open mind and heart. Know that everyone struggles with balancing and flexibility. Know that we all are built differently, even those of us with CMT. We all have different abilities. Learn to love where you are and be able to laugh at yourself. Don't be too hard on yourself. Everything in life takes work, including yoga poses and meditation. It can take a long time to undo the bad habits to which our bodies and minds have become accustomed. Be patient with yourself. A famous Hatha Yoga teacher in India said, "Practice and all is coming."

Starting the day with a morning practice is wonderful, but people in general are a lot more flexible in the evenings. After you're comfortable with a yoga practice, try it one day in the morning and another day in the evening. In the morning your mind may be more calm, focused and meditative because you're just waking up. In the evening your mind may be busier, but your body more flexible. It will depend on what time of day works best for you and want you want out of your practice.

Kim Vanderhoef

I did not write the following article. It was written by Kimberly Vanderhoef for the May/June 2015 edition of the CMTA Report. Many of us spend a lot of time and energy trying to appear "normal." I love the way this article demonstrates the importance of being open and honest about our disabilities. Thank you Kim for allowing me to use it in this book.

My Secret Disease

by K.A. Vanderhoef

I 'm 30 years old, and I've just finally confirmed that I suffer from CMT. I was 5 the first time I thought: "There is something wrong with me." My sisters were running around outside. I stood inside, throwing pieces of our pink and green play cutlery into a hula hoop on the floor. I was trying hard to keep my feet planted firmly on the ground and my body straight, as the doctor had instructed my mom to instruct me. This doctor told her my problem was that I had tight tendons. This exercise and the itchy casts they gave me to put on at night were supposed to loosen my tendons and fix my problem.

I had no way of knowing that this was the beginning of a lifelong struggle. Even worse than having a disability, though, was my inability to understand it or explain it to others. Because of that, I buried it beneath a guise of normalcy. And it became my secret disease.

Some people have visible disabilities. Some have invisible disabilities like diabetes or depression. People like me fall in between and have a disguised disability. We must decide whether to disclose our disability every time it becomes apparent, or work to keep it hidden. The choice becomes simple when the disguised disability is also undiagnosed: How can you disclose a disability when you yourself don't know what it is?

The elementary school tradition called Field Day first challenged my young perspective on the world and forced me into making these decisions. Field Day was supposed to be a day of fun outdoor competition where kids get to run around, bond with teammates and win awards for their athletic abilities. The whole school came out to watch the kickoff event, a relay race. I was the third to run the relay for my four-person group. As the kid in front of me came around the last bend, we were the second out of five teams. Everyone around me was cheering, but I was so scared I thought my heart was going to beat right out of my chest. I held out my trembling hand and waited for the baton, and as I felt it hit my palm I started to run. Within a matter of seconds, all the other kids had passed me. I ran as hard as I possibly could, but it felt like there were heavy weights on my legs. I fell so far into last place that the final relay runner for the first place team actually passed me before I could complete my lap.

We came in last place. My teammates didn't understand how I could be so slow and run so weirdly. Neither did I. I had no explanation to give them, and I was simply left wondering, "Why am I different?"

It was one of the worst days of my young life, and I hoped and prayed I would never have to do anything like that again. But I did. I had to participate in Field Day every year of elementary school. I had nightmares about it—long rows of hurdles that I knew my legs weren't capable of jumping, being forced to try and falling on my face. Worse yet, my classmates became quickly aware of my inadequacy, and they never tried to hide their disappointment if I was picked for their team.

When I graduated to middle school I thought, "Thank God I will never have to endure Field Day again." But something even worse replaced it: Annual Fitness Tests—sprints, long distance running, standing jump, running jump, and my most dreaded event, the shuttle run agility test. The worst part about these tests was that you had to do them in front of your entire grade. I couldn't have picked out a worse hell for myself.

Once I got to high school, I tried telling my gym teachers I couldn't participate in the fitness tests. But without a doctor's note, they wouldn't excuse me. I didn't have a doctor's note because I didn't have a diagnosis. I didn't have a diagnosis because I didn't have a doctor. I didn't have a doctor because I was trying so hard to ignore my physical limitations and pretend I was normal.

But deep down I knew how much my physical limitations were affecting my everyday life. I started avoiding situations where my disability would become obvious. I started skipping gym class. I avoided walking to class with my friends, taking the long way around so I could go up the ramp instead of the stairs. I became anxious when I went any place unfamiliar for fear there would be some physical obstacle I would have to conquer. Stairs became my worst enemy.

What really frightened me was the anticipation of going off to college. I had learned how to avoid the obstacles in my teenage life. But now I'd be going off to a place where I was completely unfamiliar with the landscape, the people and the way of life. While other kids on college visits considered majors and party atmospheres, I was on the lookout for any and all obstacles I'd face and formulating ways to avoid them.

It was around this time I began to notice that I was getting worse. I wasn't okay, and I needed to figure out what was wrong with me. My parents took me to a university hospital in New York City where I heard the words "Charcot-MarieTooth disease" for the first time. I thought, "What's wrong with these people? It's my legs not my teeth!"

The doctor was intrigued and invited in a slew of interns while he did a physical examination on me. It was the first, but certainly not the last, time that a doctor said that my problem was "scientifically intriguing." That's because most of the doctors I saw over the next 10 years lacked a clear understanding of Charcot-Marie-Tooth disease or how it affected me. The most I ever got out of them was, "Oh, yeah. I remember. We spent a day on that in med school."

While that first doctor told me he suspected I had CMT— which he also told me had no treatment or cure—he couldn't definitively diagnose me unless my family and I all went through genetic testing. But I learned enough to know that my leg, feet and hand muscles were deteriorating, and that nothing could change that. So in hopelessness and avoidance, I put my initial diagnosis aside until after college. But, as it often does, life got away from me, and before I knew it more than 10 years had gone by without an official diagnosis.

Although I entered college with an unofficial diagnosis, I continued to hide my disease, now with the added struggle of knowing what it meant for my future. As luck would have it, my room was on the top floor of my freshman dorm and I had to walk up three long flights of stairs numerous times a day. I continued to avoid walking up stairs with people and making excuses to linger behind after the others left (making me chronically late for classes), but it was impossible to find an excuse every single time. Toward the end of my freshman year, my roommates finally confronted me about why I had such problems going up the stairs and why I never participated in intramural sports. To my surprise, I told them the truth. And it felt amazing. I couldn't stop it from pouring out of me, and my whole body trembled with a mixture of fear, anticipation, and most of all, relief—the kind of relief that only comes from sharing a deeply held, agonizing secret.

From that point on, I didn't try to hide my struggle when I was with my friends. Whenever we went upstairs or a hill, without a word they would instinctively reach out a hand to support me. They didn't make fun of me, pity me, or question me. They gave me the title of "soccer mom" when I started coming to watch all their games from the sidelines to cheer them on, rather than pressuring me to participate. And I realized, after almost two decades of hiding, that the truth had set me free. Things got a little easier after that, and slowly the circle of people I trusted with my secret began to expand.

In the eight years since college, I've continued to struggle with social anxiety in new situations or with new people. I'm still self-conscious about my disability and still find it awkward to disclose to acquaintances or strangers. But knowing the truth about why I am the way I am, and being open to share that with others, has made it significantly easier to actually face my disease head on.

This year, through the CMTA website, I finally found a neurologist who is an expert in CMT, who took the time to understand my individual battle with it and gave me an official diagnosis. She explained how all the other physical problems I'd been dealing with stemmed from my CMT, and helped me come up with a game plan for addressing it all. And she told me that, while 10 years ago there weren't any real treatments, there is a significant amount of genetic research being done today that may lead to treatment and maybe even a cure within my lifetime. Best of all, she gave me not only a diagnosis, but a prognosis. And it wasn't all bad. While I will have to undergo permanent pain management and therapy, she told me that given the trajectory of my disease, she is convinced that I will maintain functional use of my legs and hands for the rest of my life, without the need for a wheel chair. It was the first time I'd ever cried tears of joy in a doctor's office and the first time I'd ever allowed myself hope for the future. I only wish I had confronted this and found her sooner.

I know that many people with CMT experience the same struggles, some more than I. But there is always hope for the future. While we can't control the fact that we have this disease, we can control how we respond to it. I don't want anyone, particularly the youth of today who are battling this disease in silence, to waste decades like I did, hiding from the disease, hiding from themselves and from society. Let the truth set you free. Take control of your disease. Own it, don't let it own you. And don't ever give up hope because you're not alone. Every time you face your stairs, we are all out there with you, reaching out our hands to support you and cheering you on.

4

The Strivers

"Strength does not come from physical capacity.
It comes from an indomitable will."

Ghandi

James Cuizon

There is an amazing group that I follow on Facebook called CMTAthletes. While reading the posts from this group, I was particularly impressed by the athletic accomplishments of James Cuizon. James lives in Hawaii, has CMT Type X and is a world-class physically challenged triathlete. Here is his story:

James Cuizon

James Cuizon is a busy guy. Diagnosed with CMT Type X when he was 20 years old, James currently works as the executive director of a large nonprofit organization, works part-time for another non-profit, and somehow still finds time to train and compete as a world-class physically challenged triathlete.

Born to a single mother and raised with the help of his grandmother and two uncles in Waianae, Hawaii, James knew that he was clumsy as a child, but he didn't know why. At 20, he got a job at a paint store that required him to be on his feet eight hours a day. James found the standing incredibly tiring and repeatedly asked his boss for sitting breaks. His boss advised him to see a doctor; one doctor led to another, and eventually James was diagnosed with CMT and outfitted with leg braces. The diagnosis left James stunned. He initially rebelled and threw his ankle foot orthotics (AFOs) in the trash. While he later relented and got new AFOs (this time paying out of his own pocket), James was determined not to let his CMT get in the way of his dreams.

James' first "real" job was working as an investigator for the Bank of Hawaii. The job was interesting and financially rewarding, but bad for his health. In just two years, James watched his weight balloon from 140 to 200 pounds. Determined to get his weight under control, James went online and found the CMTAthletes website (now at www.facebook.com/groups/cmta thletes). He was amazed to learn that people with CMT were competing in full-distance Ironman triathlons. He decided that if they could do it, so could he.

James started training, quickly dropping the pounds and increasing his fitness. In time, he began entering competitions. He started with a sprint triathlon, then completed the Tinman Triathlon, and by 2012 had decided to aim for the big time -- the 2013 Ironman World Championships in Kona, Hawaii.

To train for the Ironman World Championship, James competed in three races in 2012: The Dick Evans Road Race (a 112-mile bike ride), the Waikiki Rough Water Swim (2.4 miles) and the Honolulu Marathon (26.2 miles). Then it was time for an Ironman. James won a lottery slot for the Kona Ironman World Championships, but needed to complete an Ironman race to validate his slot. James' first full-distance Ironman triathlon was in Coeur d'Alene, Idaho. Only two racers showed up to compete in the Physically Challenged Division, James and a man named Edward Sproull. When Edward finished the swim with a substantial lead, James thought he was in trouble, but he managed to overtake his rival during the cycling portion and never relinquished his lead. James won first place in his division and headed to the Ironman World Championship in Kona, Hawaii!

Limited to just 2,000 athletes, the Ironman World Championship is one of the premier athletic events in the world. During the race, James reports that his thoughts were on all of the people who supported him on his journey, especially his mom, a cancer survivor, his family and all of the people affected by CMT around the world. James finished in third place in his division and made everyone in the world with CMT incredibly proud!

Recently, James was appointed as the new executive director of Network Enterprises Inc., which provides vocational rehabilitation, job training, job placement and support services to Hawaiian residents with physical, social, economic and/or intellectual/cognitive challenges. James is thrilled to be working for the good of his community and is proud to report that he has secured a new seven-figure contract for NEI that will help more people in Hawaii's disabled community land well paying jobs.

James says that his CMT presents him with challenges every day, including opening toothpaste caps, buttoning his shirt, typing, texting, working on his bike, working with knives and working with anything hot. James puts on his TurboMed* braces as soon as he gets out of bed in the morning. Despite his myriad challenges, James has big plans for the future. In addition to directing the work of the NEI, James plans to compete in the 2016 Boston Marathon (his second) and a Honu Ironman 70.3 in Hawaii in June 2016.

James advises everyone with CMT to engage in some form of exercise. In his words, "A fit body is the key to everything else. If you don't feel healthy, you won't perform at your best in any part of your life. Don't worry if others are better than you. Do the best you can. The only person you are really competing with is yourself."

* James says that before he got his TurboMed braces, he was breaking a pair of carbon fiber AFOs about every six months. He recently became a TurboMed sponsored athlete and says the braces, which he calls the best he has ever used, appear to be virtually indestructible. The company offers a two-year warranty and a 100 percent refund if returned within two months (www.turbomedorthotics.com/).

Anthony Zahn

I first heard about Anthony Zahn on Facebook, and I was immediately fascinated. I could never have imagined anyone with CMT becoming an Olympic medalist. Much to his credit, Anthony agreed almost instantly to an interview, and I have to admit I was quite the fan-boy as we talked. As with others, I was struck particularly by Anthony's tenacity in the face of diversity and never say die attitude. Here is his story:

Anthony Zahn

Anthony Zahn played soccer in kindergarten, but he wasn't great at it. As a freshman in high school, he tried to play football, but his knees hurt so badly he had to quit. Then, 15 years old and undeterred by his knee pain, Anthony took up cycling with the dream of riding in the Tour de France. It took a year and a half for a neurologist in Loma Linda, California, to realize the cause of his knee pain was CMT. Anthony brushed off the diagnosis and held onto his dream, deciding that he would be even more famous as the first man to ride in the Tour de France with a degenerative neuromuscular disease.

Anthony won the first race he ever entered, a relay triathlon in which he rode the bicycling portion of the race. He attributes that victory mostly to the other two people on his team. As time went on, Anthony began competing in bicycle road races, often finishing in the middle of the pack. Then one day, a fellow bicycle racer who had muscular dystrophy noticed Anthony's skinny legs, and they began talking. The disabled racer, a man named Ryan Levinson, recommended that Anthony get the level of his disability classified, and then race as a para-athlete. Anthony agreed, shifted his goals and kept reaching upwards.

The severity of Anthony's disability was officially classified (a requirement for a para-athlete) in July 2005, and he began competing as a disabled athlete. It took him two years to rise through the ranks to the very highest level of competition, the USA National "A" Team. In 2008, he won a coveted spot on the US Paralympic team headed to Beijing. The Paralympics are held immediately after the ablebodied Olympics, in the same venues. Anthony describes them as a big, crazy circus. The athletes, according to Anthony, have a stunning array of body types, from tiny female gymnasts to enormous male bodybuilders. Throw in disabilities of every conceivable nature, and the people watching rises to a whole new level. With the nightclubs and other distractions in the Olympic village, the trick, according to Anthony, is to soak it all in while still staying focused on your races. Anthony must have achieved the right balance because he medaled in Beijing, bringing home the Bronze in the individual time trial.

Four years later, at a World Cup race in a small town in northeast Canada, a car somehow entered the course and collided with Anthony. The collision left him with a concussion, two cracked ribs, a separated shoulder, and various other scrapes and bruises. Despite his injuries, Anthony traveled to London just six weeks later and was able to put together two eighth-place finishes in the 2012 Paralympics.

Anthony is no stranger to surgery. At 22, he had a procedure known as a "triple arthrodesis" (the fusion of three main joints) on his left foot, along with a tendon transfer. Post-surgery, Anthony was in a full leg cast for six months and a partial cast for another six months. It was more than a year before he could put a shoe on his left foot and 18 months before he could climb back on a bicycle. He has also undergone a carpal tunnel release and toe straightening procedures.

Despite the injuries and surgery, Anthony does not take any pain medications, not even ibuprofen. No fan of drugs in the first place, his concern about being suspended from racing because of a drug test made the decision even easier. Anthony does not use any special equipment, either on his bicycle or his person. The bicycles he rides are expensive but not equipped in any special way for his disability. He once had a pair of custom cycling shoes with built-in AFOs, but the constant stress quickly broke them and now he wears standard clip-ins.

On July 6, 2014, at the Road Cycling National Championships in Madison, Wisconsin, Anthony retired from bicycle racing. After a 25-year career, retiring was bittersweet. He loved the racing and his fellow racers and had medaled at every level of competition, including three bronze medals at the world championships. But he no longer had the energy for the training required to compete at a world-class level. Anthony believes that while recreational exercise can be beneficial for people with CMT, the intense training he did probably exacerbated his condition.

Today, Anthony coaches other cyclists at all levels, from weekend athletes to Paralympic hopefuls. If you are interested in benefiting from Anthony's years of cycling experience, feel free to contact him on Facebook or through his company, A to Z Cycling. Anthony Zahn has been a member of the CMTA since 2012.

For more information:

http:\\www.Facebook.com\AtoZcycling

http:\\www.facebook.com\WavestoWine

LIA O'SULLIVAN (LEADING THE PACK)

I first began writing these profiles for the CMTA newsletter, Elizabeth Ouellette suggested I contact Tau and Eoin O'Sullivan and have them share the story of their daughter, Lia. Members of Elizabeth's CMTA Branch in California, the story that Tau and Eoin related about Lia was both heartbreakihng and inspiring and the pictures of Lia they sent melted my heart. Here is their story:

Lia O'Sullivan

Vavatau Kalikau Halafihi (Tau) grew up the youngest of 11 children on the Island of Tongatapu (northeast of New Zealand) in the Kingdom of Tonga. Her parents worked hard to support their large family, and her older siblings helped raise the young ones. When Tau was just 16, her father passed away from lung cancer, and soon thereafter she followed her brother and his family to the United States. Tau describes herself as a "good girl," who as a teenager could always be found in one of three places: home, school or church.

Literally on the other side of the world, Eoin O'Sullivan was growing up in Farran, Ireland (outside of Cork City). Eoin was studious and loved to read and draw. Awarded a work placement in California while in college, Eoin fell in love with the state and soon became a resident.

A few years after arriving in the states, Eoin was in Reno, Nevada, for a friend's bachelor party. Playing poker in a casino at 3:00 am, he looked up to see a tall, exotically beautiful woman standing nearby. In his mind, he had hit the jackpot. When she left, he literally ran after her. They stayed up talking all night, and although Tau lived in Sacramento and Eoin was in San Jose, they began seeing each other every weekend. Four years later, they tied the knot.

A few years after their marriage, Tau gave birth to a beautiful baby girl they named Sesilia Deirdre O'Sullivan (Lia). For the first six months of her life, Lia seemed to be growing and developing in a normal fashion. But when Lia showed no signs of walking at 12 months, her parents began to grow concerned. Although her doctors at Kaiser Permanente insisted she was fine, Eoin and Tau were not convinced. In addition to not walking, Lia also showed signs of hyper-flexibility and had a twitch in one eye. These conditions drew the doctor's attention, and eventually Lia was given a nerve conduction test. Genetic testing confirmed that Lia had CMT Type 1B. According to her doctors, there is only one other person in the world with Lia's exact mutation.

For Eoin and Tau, learning that Lia had CMT was almost a relief. While they were concerned that CMT was serious and degenerative, there were other possibilities that could have been far worse, even fatal. Searching for information about CMT online, Eoin and Tau found the CMTA website and soon went to their first CMTA Support and Action Group meeting, led by SAG Facilitator and CMTA Board Member Elizabeth Ouellette. At 2 years of age, Lia was by far the youngest person at the meeting, but the welcome was warm and the group was "lovely." As chance would have it, one person at the meeting was Dr. John W. Day from Stanford University Hospital. Stanford is a Center of Excellence for the treatment of CMT, and Dr. Day soon became Lia's neurologist.

While Eoin and Tau received great support from the CMTA, their battles were not over. When it was time for Lia to attend preschool, they were told she would have to attend special education classes, populated for the most part with developmentally disabled students with mental impairment. Because Lia is a particularly bright and social young girl, Eoin and Tau feared special education classes would restrict her educational and social opportunities. With the help of friends who provided guidance and helped them learn their rights, Eoin and Tau were able to have Lia reassessed and then reassigned to a standard classroom environment.

Today, Lia is three years old and attends standard preschool classes with a state-provided aide who assists her with tasks and looks out for her safety. She also goes to weekly physical and occupational therapy sessions. Lia wears braces (AFOs to her ankles) and has a walker—although when she wants to get somewhere fast, the walker is often abandoned. She has visited Tonga and Ireland several times. Every four to six months, Lia sees Dr. John Day and the entire team at Stanford.

Lia's favorite book is Everyone has Something by CMTA Advisory Board Member Sarah Kesty. She has a signed copy and insists on having it read to her almost every night. Having CMT has never slowed Lia down. In the words of her father, "Lia is the most determined kid you will ever meet. She has never made a fuss about falling. She just dusts herself off and gets moving. Her spirit is incredible."

5

The Thrivers

"Surviving is important. Thriving is elegant."

Maya Angelou

Jim Moneyhon

Jim Moneyhon is more than just a friend and a fellow CMTA Baltimore Branch member. Jim is a role model for me as I age and my CMT progresses. If I can accommodate my CMT with one tenth the good humor, acceptance, and ingenuity that Jim does I will be a very happy man. My nickname for Jim is Professor Gadget because he has an entire tool kit full of devices that allow him to accomplish everyday tasks despite his CMT. Here is his story:

Jim Moneyhon

When Jim Moneyhon finds something he likes, he sticks with it. Hired by the Navy at the age of 22 to work at the Naval Weapons Lab in rural Dahlgren, Virginia, James has remained in the same job, in the same building, for the last 46 years. A physicist by training and a tinkerer by nature, Jim has found a number of unique ways to work around his CMT and continue working at a job he enjoys in a town he has never found a reason to leave.

Born in the Philadelphia suburbs and educated in Gettysburg, Pennsylvania, Jim moved to the tiny town of Dahlgren right after college. When he met a local girl and they decided to tie the knot, the natural location was the base chapel. A few years later, Jim and his wife were the proud parents of six boys and girls (three biological and three adopted).

Jim was about 45 and working on a ship at sea when he first noticed the symptoms that were later diagnosed as CMT. He found himself constantly walking in small circles in an effort to maintain his balance, an unusual dance that no one else on board seemed to be performing. A visit to a series of doctors, including an ENT and an orthopedist, eventually led to a neurologist and resulted in a diagnosis of CMT Type 2.

In the years since his diagnosis, Jim has found a number of ingenious ways to work around his disease. In the late 90s, Jim attended a disability exposition in Chantilly, Virginia, and purchased a device called an EZ Chair. Essentially a wheelchair with pedals, the EZ Chair was maneuverable, comfortable, lightweight, and could be easily folded and stored. Jim describes it as a "lifesaver." In a job that required a lot of travel, the EZ Chair could be used to carry a laptop and a briefcase, and on an airplane it could be easily folded and stored. The pedals also offered a great form of exercise.

Sadly, the EZ Chair is no longer manufactured, but Jim has taken extraordinary measures to keep his two chairs up and running. When an airline employee accidently broke the chair's front axle, Jim was able to build a temporary splint with parts from Home Depot. Later, his oldest son took it to an aluminum welder who fixed and reinforced the broken portion of the chair. Jim recently rode his chair into a meeting of the Baltimore CMTA Branch, where it was an immediate object of great interest. Jim reports that it attracts women and children "like driving a Camaro."

In addition to the EZ Chair, Jim has a number of devices that make his life with CMT much easier. These include Hikker brand hiking poles (available on Amazon.com)—to which he added Pace Maker rubber tips for increased stability and traction, the Pocket Dresser (which has several button hooks and an attachment for managing zippers), and, to help him with eating, a Rocking T-Knife for cutting food. He carries a pair of Gerber pliers with him on his belt—they're springloaded, and are good for picking up and gripping things that he can't manage otherwise due his lack of manual dexterity. Another tool that he has found quite useful is a pair of Black & Decker electric scissors (sadly no longer made). Jim's wife is an avid reader and always keeps her eyes peeled for other products that Jim might find helpful. Jim uses Version 12 of Dragon Naturally Speaking software at work and is learning the intricacies of Version 13 at home. Although he says he hasn't yet learned to utilize all of its capabilities, Dragon has been a great help in transcribing his written notes, since his handwriting is not particularly legible.

After experiencing several instances of stumbling and falling while on naval ships, Jim no longer visits them at sea. But he still finds his work with the Navy and the Department of Defense interesting and important, and he has no immediate plans for retirement. (His wife jokes that they will carry him out of his office in a pine box.)

JIM MONEYHON'S GADGETS FOR FOLK'S WITH CMT

Dressing & Personal Care

Button hook

Pocket Dresser

Over-the-calf socks (crew and dress)

Safety razor—Gillette ProFusion (Heavy handle easier to grip and hold)

Shower seat/bench (Carex Universal Bath Bench with Back)

Suction cup shower handle

Nail clip (Trim Easy Hold Toenail, rubber-covered)

Hair brush (instead of comb)—Rubber handle, cylindrical, with bristles (Sally's Beauty Supply)

Mobility

Walking Stick (Hikker) HP-5 Anti-Shock Hiking Pole, 2-pack

Rubber Tips—Pace Maker Extended Life Vulcanized Tips

EZ Chair (Premier Designs, Fresno, CA)

TravelScoot

Collapsible Cart (Staples, Office Depot)

Magna-Cart Hand Truck

Computers, SmartPhones, and Software

Dragon Naturally Speaking (Nuance) (Version 13)

iPhone

Dragon Apps

Vlingo

Stylus

Tools/Manipulators

Gerber Pliers (Spring-Loaded)

Hemostats

Clothespins

Non-skid tape (for iPhone connectors, etc.)

Office Supplies

Letter openers (Razor-Blade)

Scissors—Black and Decker Electric (Out of Production?)

Scissors—Fiskars EA0611 (Multi-Function with Holster)

Scissors—Zibra ZPCOPEN-OR Universal Package Opener

Kitchen

Can opener KitchenAid (Large crank handle)

One touch can opener (Battery Powered)—Requires LOTS of batteries!!

Lids-Off (Black and Decker Electric, 110 VAC)

Kitchen scissors (poultry shears)—Good Cook "Touch"

Hamilton Beach Open Ease Automatic Jar Opener

Salt/Pepper Grinder (Chef'n)

Bottle/Jar Opener

> Black—Progressive 6-in-1 Multi Opener (GT-2950KM)
> Green—Kitchen Kahuna Silicone Easy Jar Opener
> Rubber hand gripping mats
> Plastic-Rubber Top
> Pampered Chef Bottle/Jar Opener (Y-Shaped)

2-Liter Bottle Pouring Handle

Dining/Eating

Rocking T-Knife

Crab Leg Tool (Chef'n)

Mugs-are-better-than-Glasses (Handles)

Household (and Auto) Cleaning

Swiffers

Wash Mitt

Dust Mitt

Window Squeegee (Ettore)

Around the House

3-Step Stool with Hand-Rail (Cosco)

Velcro Straps and Strips (General Purpose)

Bungee Cords

<u>Shopping</u>

Haul-Helper Carabiner

Use store handicap scooters—they are there for you!

<u>Miscellaneous Coping Skills [Focus on The Things You CAN Do, and Apply Them To Things That You Can't]</u>

Pants/dress hangers (use strongest portion of your hand)

Screw-type bottle tops—Squeeze with strongest part of hand and fingers

Aron Taylor

Marcia once heard Pat Livney refer to a singer/songwriter with CMT, and when she first mentioned him to me, I was immediately intrigued, and set about tracking him down. It did not take much time on Google to find him. Aron Taylor is a guy who has been passionately following his own muse for years and his efforts have culminated in some really fine music. Here is his story:

Aron Taylor

Born into a music-loving family, some of singer/songwriter Aron Taylor's earliest memories are of listening to Led Zeppelin and Pink Floyd albums in the living room of his home in Parsons, Kansas.

While still in grade school, Aron discovered hip-hop and was soon reciting lyrics that reminded him of tongue twisters or nursery rhymes.

In second grade, Aron's parents noticed that he ran with an awkward gait. They took him to the doctor, who diagnosed him with Charcot-Marie-Tooth disease.

When I was just a tyke
My momma saw me running in the street
And something didn't look right

In fifth grade, Aron was fitted with plastic leg braces. They pinched when he played kickball and he tried to remove them, but his teacher stopped him. That same year Aron had surgery on his legs and he entered sixth grade in a wheelchair.

When the surgeon finally removed the casts from his legs, Aron's leg muscles had atrophied. The doctor told him that the muscles would never return. This encounter forever damaged Aron's perspective of doctors, and he hasn't worn braces or seen a doctor about his CMT since.

Aron suffered a lot of anxiety and self-consciousness as a result of his CMT, and frequently wondered if people were staring at him and noticing that he was "different." But despite his anxieties, Aron never lost his love of music, and by eighth grade he was writing his own songs.

Feeling isolated on an island

Took a pen and started writing

Desperate to produce his own music but unsure what equipment he needed, Aron one day dialed 411 and asked for the number for a "DJ store in New York City." To his amazement, this gambit worked and he soon possessed a catalog of musical recording equipment. Aron bought his first equipment and went into production.

In 1998, he released a CD that he created in its entirety, from cover art to printing. He sold it around Parsons and neighboring towns. In 2002, he produced his first professional album entitled "Ridiculous Beats Presents: BOOM!!! Midwest Ballaz," that is still available on iTunes (https://itunes.apple.com/us/album/ridiculous-beatspresents/id65109674). In 2010, Aron released "Lovefest," a hiphop/rap album with 21 of his own songs. In 2013, Aron decided to look inward and began writing songs about overcoming obstacles, including his own. While his previous work was frequently sarcastic and tongue-in-cheek, the new music was more serious and focused on delivering a message. The effort produced Aron's finest work to-date, including a song entitled "The Life You Love," in which Aron sings candidly about his own battle with CMT.

Ya gotta get up and get to it
Overcome your fears and make no excuses

While Aron is hopeful that his music might one day become a full-time job, he is practical enough to have a good career already in place as an IT professional at a law firm. Recently married, Aron walks a lot, lifts weights and recently lost about 15 pounds. Aron has had his share of falls and injuries, but he finds that staying active is the best prescription, and that staying fit not only minimizes falls but reduces the injuries he suffers when the inevitable falls occur. Aron is a big fan of the CMTA's various forums on Facebook and believes they offer great advice to both those with CMT and those living with someone who has CMT.

More information on Aron and his music can be found on www.ridiculousbeats.com. He also hosts two weekly online radio shows on a website called LawrenceHits.com. One of them is called The Hip-Hop Happy Hour (H4), which airs at 6 p.m. CST every Wednesday. The other is a show on Thursdays at 6 p.m. CST called Ridiculous Rock (R2) and features mostly classic rock.

Vickie says CMT bugs us all....

Vicki Halfyard

What is it like to have CMT? What does it feel like? How does it impact one emotionally? Many of us who have the disease struggle in describing it to others. Those of us who are writers try to put our experiences and our daily challenges into words. Some people take another route. I first encountered Vicki's work on Facebook and was struck by the unique way in which she related her personal experiences. Here is Vicki's story:

Vicki Halfyard

Vicki Halfyard is an artist living in Michigan who has found a unique means of sharing her CMT experiences. Vicki uses an app on Facebook, along with an avatar and storyboards to share her daily CMT experiences with the world. In her frequent Facebook posts, Vicki's shows her avatar encountering difficulties with stairs, dark rooms, hand coordination, falls and all kinds of other situations. Vicki's facial expression and a caption below succinctly capture her feelings.

While Vicki has always had CMT symptoms, only in the last six months has she received a CMT diagnosis, and her recent posts show her avatar rejoicing in finally knowing the cause of her problems and finding others who share them.

Born in the suburbs of Detroit, Vicki began manifesting symptoms of CMT at just 8 years old. These symptoms were similar to those encountered by her grandfather, her mother and two of three siblings. The cause was unknown. As a young woman, Vicki loved to dance, and her passion led her to a job running a dance studio. Unfortunately, her physical condition and her vocation were not matched, and at 24 Vicki fractured her ankle and was forced to give up the job she loved.

While she remained a self-described "junkie for dance," Vicki pursued other occupations, including car sales and grocery store deli worker. During this time, she experienced all the typical CMT symptoms, including foot drop, hand tremors and fatigue, but was consistently misdiagnosed with multiple sclerosis and other ailments. Vicki regularly left her doctor's office in tears. In addition to her CMT ailments, Vicki also appears to have some unique symptoms, such as visual disturbances causing a strobe light sensation, temporary colorblindness and sound sensitivities. Despite all these issues, Vicki has a lighthearted attitude towards life.

Vicki's recent diagnosis has brought her some peace of mind and enjoyment in discovering the larger CMT community. Now 58, she is retired and survives the long Michigan winters by curling up in her jammies and watching old movies. Vicki reports that she still dances in her dreams.

Note: Vicki's doctors recently informed her she does not have CMT, but a neurological problem with similar symptoms.

6

The Activists

"How wonderful it is that nobody need wait a single moment before starting to improve the world."

Anne Frank

Patrick Livney

Patrick Livney

Pat Livney is the man most responsible for building the Charcot-Marie-Tooth Association into a robust, active and focused organization. At the helm of the CMTA since 2008, Pat has grown the organization more than tenfold while focusing its resources on the STAR initiative and its goal of finding a cure for CMT. The son of immigrants who came to this country chasing the American dream, Pat is dedicated to the mission of the CMTA and the work that he describes as both noble and tremendously rewarding.

An all-around athlete in his youth, Patrick grew up playing soccer and baseball. He also wrestled and boxed. At the age of 16, Pat broke his left ankle, which healed and then broke again. Shortly thereafter Patrick was told he had Charcot-Marie-Tooth disease, but he refused to believe the diagnosis.

In search of answers, Patrick traveled all the way to Hungary and Luxembourg to consult with neurological experts before finally arriving at Columbia Presbyterian Hospital in New York. There he was told that he would be in a wheelchair before the age of 30 and that he should focus his energies on developing his mind rather than his body. While the wheelchair diagnosis was way off the mark, Patrick regards the admonition to develop his mind as the best advice he ever received.

Depressed with his diagnosis, and still in partial denial, Patrick transferred among a few schools before earning an engineering degree from Roosevelt University in Chicago. During this time, Patrick tripped intermittently, walked like a cowboy and couldn't help noticing that his legs were thinning. Anxious to focus his energies on the positive, Patrick began raising funds for the Muscular Dystrophy Association and volunteering for them as a camp counselor.

To earn a living, Patrick began working on Wall Street, first as an institutional bond trader and later as an asset manager. One evening he was in Michael Jordan's restaurant in Grand Central Station when a guy walked by carrying a tray of shots. After observing Patrick's legs and gait and shaking his hand, the stranger informed Patrick that he appeared to have Charcot-Marie... Patrick finished the sentence for him. The stranger turned out to be Chris O'Donnell, whose own family has been afflicted by Charcot-Marie-Tooth disease. Chris told Patrick that he needed to meet his brother, Steve O'Donnell, who was on the board of the CMTA. In short order, Patrick met Steve and Dr. Michael Shy, secured a $250,000 donation from the Livney Foundation, and joined the CMTA board.

At his second CMTA board meeting, while discussing a $300,000 multi-year research grant, Pat asked what would happen if the research proved unsuccessful in year one. Would the CMTA still continue funding the research? He was told that it would, illuminating a process that Pat felt was flawed. In time, this and other issues led to an off-site meeting in California, the formation of a scientific advisory board, the Strategy to Accelerate Research (STAR), and ultimately to Pat's promotion to CMTA CEO.

Patrick says that leading the work of the CMTA is the most rewarding thing he has ever done (with the exceptions of his marriage and the birth of his daughter). He says that it feels awesome to be part of a collaborative effort working for such a noble cause, but that his mission will not be complete until there is a pill for at least one CMT subtype and a methodology for finding medications for the others.

Patrick has also worked hard to ensure that the CMTA will receive some of the economic benefit that could result from the discovery of a drug for CMT. A "seat at the table" could help ensure the future funding of the CMTA if a drug for some of the more common subtypes is developed first.

In his spare time, Patrick has married his hobby of golf with his CMTA fundraising mission by creating an annual golf tournament. In the nine years the tournament has been in existence, it has raised in excess of $2 million dollars for the CMTA.

Hayley, Jeana, and Rylee Sweeny

As the CMTA Director of Community Service, Jeana is one of the most well-known people in the CMTA. Everyone knows Jeana. But how many people know her personal story, and the many trials and tribulations she has faced in her still young life? Here is her story:

Jeana Sweeny

Born into a family of six children, Jeana was always the klutz. She fell frequently. In the emergency room of the local hospital, they knew her by name. At the age of 15, she was taken to Children's Hospital in Pittsburgh where a local doctor had her roll up her pants leg and walk up and down the hall. Within five minutes, the doctor suspected she had CMT. A nerve conduction study confirmed the diagnosis.

At 16, Jeana had triple arthrodesis surgery on both feet, one after the other. While Jeana knew little about her disease, and hoped that the surgery might take care of everything, her surgeon gave three horrifying orders that would ring in her ears for years: **Jeana can't go to gym class. Jeana can't work. Jeana can't have children.** Jeana ignored her doctor and planned on doing all three.

Hoping to put the doctor's prognosis behind her, Jeana found a job and started dating. One day Jeana and a boy she was dating went skiing. After a half hour on the slopes, Jeana began feeling a sharp pain and burning sensations in her feet. They raced back to the lodge, Jean ripped off her boots and observed with horror that her feet were ice cold. She freaked out, began rubbing her feet frantically, and rocking back and forth. Jeana's feet recovered, but her date did not. She never heard from the boy again.

After her disastrous ski date, Jeana's mother advised her to begin telling people about her CMT. It was not long after this that Jeana met Chris Sweeny, and fell hopelessly in love. Determined to tell him about her CMT, Jeana invited him to a homemade lasagna dinner complete with garlic bread and wine and informed him she had funky feet and weak leg muscles. Chris shrugged off the news and later proposed.

In 2002, Jeana heard about a CMTA support group forming in Johnstown, Pennsylvania. This was big news. Jeana had always felt that she was the only person in the world with CMT. Now it turned out she was not even the only person in Johnstown! Jeana went to the meeting with a million questions. She decided to get involved and begin fundraising. As Jeana soon learned, there is no manual for raising money for a non-profit like the CMTA. You try everything, and you go with what works. She believes that if you are trying, then you are not failing. If you touch even just one person, you are making a difference.

Jeana's first little lady, Hayley, was born in 2000. Hayley has never been tested for CMT and shows no signs of the disease. Hayley is athletic, intelligent, and happy to help open jars or do anything else to help her mom. In fifth grade she even won a balancing contest. Jeana was so happy she wanted to throw a party. Things went so well with Hayley that by the time of her second pregnancy, Jeana was relaxed and confident that she could take on any challenge. Then life threw her a curve ball.

Rylee Sweeny was born in 2005. When nurses handed her daughter to Jeana minutes after her birth, Jeana immediately noticed that she wasn't breathing right and asked the doctors to examine her. After a cursory examination, the doctors handed her back to Jeana. The pattern repeated.

While still in the hospital, Rylee turned blue. Jeana screamed for help. They managed to revive her and then sent them both home. Eventually, Rylee was diagnosed with Congenital Pulmonary Lymphangiectasia (CPL), a rare condition with a frequently high mortality rate. Jeana swore she would not lose her daughter.

While running a diagnostic genetic test on Rylee, doctors discovered that she also had CMT. On hearing the news, Jeana felt like someone had punched her in the gut. Children with CPL are at high risk for respiratory infections. In order to protect her daughter, Jeana covered all the sofas in her house, had Chris change out of his USPS uniform before entering the house, severely limited all house guests, and required those who were allowed to enter the house to learn CPR. Despite all Jeana's precautions, Riley eventually did get an infection and had to spend a month in the hospital.

Despite all the challenges, Jeana loves being a mom and her "little ladies" mean everything to her. She has been right there with them through every challenge and she loves them so much that it hurts. When Rylee was three years old, the STAR program (Strategy to Accelerate Research) was born. Jeana reports that knowing this program is in place means the world to her.

Jeana continues to work her heart out every day for the CMTA and she encourages everyone reading this to join the CMTA, hold a fundraiser, and consider becoming a CMTA Branch Leader. Both Hayley and Rylee are currently thriving.

Jonah Berger

Jonah Berger comes from a large family with CMT Type X. Jonah's grandmother had it and passed the genes to three of her four daughters. Those three daughters had a total of nine children, three of whom now have CMT. CMTA Board Member Steve Weiss is Jonah's first cousin. Here is Jonah's story:

Jonah Berger

Born in Rockville, Maryland, Jonah's mother was the first person in the family to be diagnosed with CMT. Jonah was diagnosed soon after, when he was just 5. One of the few things that Jonah remembers is screaming at the top of his lungs during the EMT. Jonah also remembers his father sitting him down and drawing a picture of the human body as he tried to explain how the nervous system worked and how the messages from his brain might have trouble always reaching his feet.

In his mid-teens, Jonah began tripping and losing his balance frequently. His running was awkward. While his physical issues were noticeable, Jonah says the psychological ones were much harder to deal with. Jonah just wanted to be "normal."

When he was 18, an orthotist recommended that Jonah wear braces. Pride, vanity and an aversion to appearing different kept Jonah brace-free. Finally, at the age of 23, an orthotist convinced Jonah to simply try on a pair of AFOs and walk across the office. Jonah put them on and had what he describes as a "magic moment." He began walking and suddenly realized he no longer had to concentrate on lifting his feet. He walked across the office, out the door and across the parking lot before shouting at his doctor "Make me a pair!"

Shortly after earning a graduate degree in special education Jonah had a dream that he was lost deep in the woods in the Rocky Mountains of Colorado. He came upon a cabin and knocked on the door. Stephanie, an old friend from high school, answered the door and invited him in, rescuing Jonah from certain death in the frozen north woods. When he awoke, Jonah tracked down Stephanie, whom he had not heard from in nearly a decade, only to discover that that just two days earlier she had moved to ... Colorado! Recognizing that the universe was sending a message that should not be ignored, Jonah soon relocated to the Mile High City.

In Colorado, Jonah found work as the director of a camp for kids with special needs, and started a company called "The Rhythm Within," which offers therapeutic mentoring to special-needs kids and adults. Through The Rhythm Within, Jonah uses community-based activities to coach and counsel folks of all ages and disabilities in how to overcome and work around their disabilities to attain their life goals and live a rich and fulfilling life.

After sharing his life story with his classmates in grad school, Jonah was encouraged to put his experiences into a book. Jonah took the advice and wrote *He Walks Like a Cowboy* over the course of the next six months. This non-fiction work perfectly encompasses the CMT experience and continues to be a must-read for those recently diagnosed with this neurologic disease.

Today, Jonah serves as a member of the CMTA Advisory Board and attends many of the Patient/Family Conferences held across the country. Jonah is the co-leader of many of the youth outings that accompany these conferences. In his spare time, Jonah enjoys camping, concerts and cooking.

Jonah advises everyone with CMT or any other disability to be open about their issues. "Never be ashamed, closeted, or quiet about what you are experiencing," he says, adding, "People are naturally curious, and should be encouraged to ask you about the challenges you face. Every question you receive is an opportunity to educate people about CMT or any other issue. Also, never let your limitations have the final word. You can accomplish anything to which you set your mind." Despite his CMT, Jonah has climbed the highest mountain in Colorado, biked across Iowa, and completed a triathlon against the advice of all of his doctors. His best advice to those with CMT: "You can do anything if you are allowed to do it in your way! Do not try to be normal, just be you!"

The Waves

The waves come crashing on the sand
What shall we do? Run for dry land?
Or take our chances and lift our feet
And ride the tide, our fortunes to meet.

We wake up each and every day
To work, and plan, and dream, and play
And strive not to trip or stumble or fall
Our pride intact, our confidence tall.

But the truth comes shining through you see
We have challenges to face, we have CMT.
Our feet are funky, our balance unsure
Our weakened hands are reaching for a cure.

And while we wait for the cure to arrive
We must challenge our fears, we must constantly strive
To teach those around us with the way we face
This challenge with strength and truth and grace.

Try not to be normal, seek not who to blame
Don't add to the weight of your feet with your shame.
Walk your own way, stumble with style
Do more than survive this, thrive this and smile
Go beyond the boundary where your comfort ends
You'll be strengthened by the wisdom it lends
And when the waves come crashing, do your best to be brave
Lift your feet and ride the wave....

—Jonah Berger

Yohan & Elizabeth

I first met Elizabeth Ouellette at a CMTA Patient/Family Conference in Orlando, Florida. In the many times our paths have crossed since, I have always been inspired by the energy and the passion both she and her brother Chris Ouellette bring to their work for the CMTA. For the past two years, my wife and I have driven up to Vermont for the annual Cycle4CMT that Elizabeth and Chris organize. It is a wonderful event and will no doubt grow and get better every year. I encourage everyone to go. Here is Elizabeth's story:

Elizabeth Ouellette

Elizabeth Ouellette has neuropathy, but she does not have CMT. In fact, before the birth of her son, Yohan, Elizabeth had never heard of Charcot-Marie-Tooth disease.

When Yohan was around 4 years old, Elizabeth and her husband began noticing that he was frequently tired and that he walked mostly on his toes. When Elizabeth took her son to the doctor, she was informed that she was putting her own pain on her child and was instructed to give Yohan a quarter for every time he walked on his heels rather than his toes. The incentive had little impact.

Over the next few years Elizabeth continued to watch her son struggle with ordinary childhood tasks like riding a bike or climbing the monkey bars. When Yohan was around 6 years old, he visited a neurologist, who diagnosed him as either having CMT or cerebral palsy. Only months later did a genetic test confirm that Yohan had a spontaneous case of CMT 1A.

The first issue that Elizabeth and her husband Gilles confronted was what to tell Yohan about his condition. While some members of her family advised Elizabeth not to say anything to her 7-year-old son, she decided to give him little bits of information at a time and found this approach worked well.

Another issue that kids with CMT face is bullying. To demonstrate what living with CMT is like, Elizabeth made a DVD in which she gave each of the kids in Yohan's fifth-grade class a pair of socks and a button-down shirt. She instructed them to put the socks on their hands and then try to button the shirt. To better mimic reality, Elizabeth heightened the stress by shouting "Hurry, hurry, the bus is coming!"

In order to stretch Yohan's Achilles tendon, so he could walk on his heels, doctors performed a procedure called serial casting. Every two weeks, Yohan's feet and lower legs were put in new plaster casts that pulled the front of his foot increasingly upward. While Yohan had previously struggled with his perceived lack of athleticism, the plaster casts gave him immediate credibility. He was allowed to pick their color and all his friends signed the casts. Unfortunately, the doctors never told Elizabeth that serial casting should be followed up by braces or night splints, and they ended up repeating the procedure three times. By the end of the third serial casting, Yohan's leg muscles had atrophied and Yohan was experiencing neuropathy and burning sensations on the bottom of his feet.

As Elizabeth struggled with Yohan's CMT, she slowly became more involved with the CMTA. Her involvement began 12 years ago with a subscription to the newsletter. She read about a woman who sent a letter to all her friends and relatives explaining her CMT diagnosis and requesting a donation for the CMTA. Elizabeth thought this was a great idea and began her own fundraising campaign. She contacted everyone she knew, told them about Yohan and his struggle with CMT and requested a donation. Elizabeth ended up raising $9,000, and sent the checks to the CMTA along with a letter explaining what she had done. Elizabeth's letter elicited a phone call from one of the CMTA's earliest employees, Pat Dreibelbis, who asked Elizabeth to write an article about her fundraising event. This, according to Elizabeth, was her "point of no return."

Thirteen years ago, just as Elizabeth finished her Master's Degree in Psychology she was asked to start a CMTA support group in the San Francisco area. It was at the first meeting of this group that Yohan first met another person with CMT. Although the other person was an 80-year-old woman, Yohan bonded with her immediately over their shared dislike of CMT and wearing braces. Elizabeth ran the support group for 10 years and describes the experience as one of the most rewarding of her life.

Nine years ago, in recognition for all that she has done for the organization, Elizabeth was asked to join the CMTA Board of Directors. Believing that she was put on this earth to do more, Elizabeth accepted. In 2007, Elizabeth and Gilles organized a strategic planning meeting with the CMTA Board of Directors in Palo Alto, California. This meeting was the genesis for the STAR program. Excited about this new approach, Elizabeth and Gilles set up a research fund to help kickstart the funding of STAR shortly thereafter.

Elizabeth's first assignment was to grow the CMTA support groups. When she began her work, the CMTA had 15 groups. Within just a few years, Elizabeth had written the CMTA support group guide, grown the number of support groups to 56, and hired Jeana Sweeney, who has since taken the support groups to a whole new level (there are now some 80 CMTA branches throughout North America).

Today, Elizabeth is Vice Chair of the CMTA Board of Directors, with a full plate of responsibilities. She provides direction and elbow grease in a number of areas, including CMTA Patient Family Conferences, the CMTA social media campaign, and CMTA leadership conferences. Yohan is currently in his senior year at Pitzer College, where he is studying to be an industrial psychologist. Yohan has inherited Elizabeth's gift for fundraising. In 2015, his "Go Blue for CMT" campaign raised some $20,000 for the CMTA. This past summer he worked as a CMTA intern and wrote A Guide to Surviving College for CMTers.

Despite her busy schedule, Elizabeth has also found the time to help one very special person. Three years ago, she received an e-mail from a 32-year-old man in India named Anand Patki. Anand had a very bad case of CMT for which he had not been properly treated. Pictures and videos revealed that he was essentially walking on his ankles and in great pain. As a testament to her passion and dedication, Elizabeth worked tirelessly to find a specialist in India who could treat Anand. Though her initial efforts were fruitless, Elizabeth pushed forward and finally, through CMTA Advisory Board Member Dr. Glenn Pfeffer, found a surgeon in India who was willing to see Anand. Today, Anand has had ankle fusion and has begun the difficult task of learning how to walk again. Anand is tremendously grateful for all the time Elizabeth has dedicated to helping him, and is hopeful he will be walking on the bottoms of his feet in the very near future.

7

The Scientists

"The important thing is to never stop questioning."

Albert Einstein

Dr. Brittany Wright, Dr. James Inglese and Dr. Trish Dranshak at the NIH.

There is amazing research on CMT going in labs on all over the world. Much of this research happens in the United States, funded by the CMTA. I was fortunate to be invited on a tour of one such facility in my home state of Maryland. Here is what I wrote about that visit:

The National Center for Advancing Translational Sciences

At a state-of-the-art laboratory in suburban Washington, D.C., a team of dedicated scientists, some of them handpicked by the CMTA, is rapidly testing hundreds of thousands of drug compounds on tiny samples of CMT-impacted cells. The scientists work for the National Center for Advancing Translational Sciences (NCATS), in Rockville, Maryland, and they are in the process of identifying compounds capable of stopping the progression of specific types of CMT. As the list of compounds that show promise as a possible drug treatment for each type of CMT is winnowed down, each candidate's characteristics are carefully examined, and some candidates are eliminated due to their toxicity, stability or other characteristics. Once a final handful of the most promising compounds is identified, animal and human trials can commence. FDA approval for a drug to arrest the progression of CMT1A is the CMTA's first goal, one that gets closer every day.

On a recent tour of NCATS, a group of CMT-affected individuals and family members witnessed firsthand the remarkable technology and amazing individuals working around the clock to achieve the CMTA's long-sought-after vision of a world without CMT. The tour began with Dr. James Inglese, head of the Laboratory of Assay Development and Screening Technology at NCATS, who provided an overview of the lab's efforts to find a treatment for CMT. Before any compounds could be tested for their ability to arrest a CMT subtype, a model of that type of CMT had to be created, miniaturized and duplicated hundreds of thousands of times to create environments in which to place the candidate compounds. These environments are known as assays, and the center in Rockville partnered with STAR project team members at Dr. John Svaren's laboratory at the University of Wisconsin to create and test these assays. Because NCATS is part of the National Institutes of Health, a part of the federal government, these assays were then made available to CMTA partners interested in testing additional compounds for their ability to halt the progression of CMT. One lab that has taken advantage of this is Genzyme, a Sanofi Company, which in February completed testing the 1.9 million compounds in its library for their impact on CMT 1A. By November,

81

2015 Genzyme had whittled that number down to a handful that could be taken to human clinical trials.

At our first lab stop on the tour, most of us expected to see row after row of test tubes, similar to the ones we worked with in our high school chemistry classes. Instead, we were informed that test tubes were largely a thing of the past, replaced by "plates" that each contain more than a thousand "wells." In each well was a tiny sample of PMP22 (approximately 2,000 cells), the protein that is overproduced in people with CMT Type 1A. Each plate costs about eight dollars, a sum that seems trivial until you realize that the center uses thousands of them at a time.

The highlight of the tour was the robotics room. Here, in a glass-enclosed room the size of a semi-trailer, huge robotic arms move trays of plates, rapidly injecting compounds into their tiny wells. The speed with which this process is performed is mind-boggling, and the work goes on 24 hours a day. Managing the robotics during our tour was Pepper Bouney, a lean, heavily tattooed former bicycle mechanic whose skills and dedication mesh perfectly with this job's requirements. He says that working on high-end bicycles for 20 years was great training for the robots. Pepper is on call at all times and is frequently summoned by the robot at odd hours to fix minor snafus.

Once compounds are injected into the tray wells with their tiny samples of CMT, they must be observed to take note of their impact on the disease. This is accomplished through a luminescent "reporter" that is added to the well plates. When a compound impacts the CMT, the reporter begins to glow. Virtually undetectable by the human eye, the amount of glow is precisely measured by more machines, which then generate spreadsheets of numbers for Trish and Brittany to analyze. Back in the lab, Trish and Brittany showed us a plate that demonstrated the various levels of light and dark that could be attained in the wells on a plate. The shades of light and dark on this particular plate had been arranged to form a replication of a head shot of Pat Livney. It was an amazing demonstration of the sensitivity of the tools for measuring compound impacts.

After a full morning of walking all over the NCATS campus, those of us lucky enough to have taken the tour were physically exhausted but mentally exhilarated by the cutting-edge science and dedicated scientists working tirelessly to find a cure for CMT. For me, the tour served as a reminder of the level of effort and size of the costs needed to finally put an end to CMT. For my friends and my family, I took the opportunity to rededicate myself to raising funds to fight for a cure. I hope you will do the same.

Brittany Wright

Young, energetic, dedicated and smart as a whip, Dr. Brittany Wright is just one of today's scientists racing to find a treatment for CMT. In her lab at NIH, or at CMTA Patient/Family conferences around the country, Brittany is that rare scientist who is both deeply engaged in the minutia of her research, and yet outgoing and fully able to explain her work in terms a layman can easily understand. Here is her story:

Brittany Wright

Born in Ashville, North Carolina, Brittany always loved dolphins and dreamed from an early age of becoming a marine biologist. With that dream in mind she headed off to Eckert College in St. Petersburg, Florida, and began her studies. While she loved biology, Brittany also loved chemistry, and half way through school switched from marine biology to marine chemistry and obtained her Bachelor of Science degree in chemistry.

Brittany attended graduate school at the University of North Carolina in Chapel Hill, where she dug into the molecular mechanisms of pain in the hope of finding a new therapeutic target. At UNC she gained valuable experience with high-throughput screening in the search for an inhibitor of the therapeutic target she had previously identified in her studies. After receiving her Ph.D. in pharmaceutical sciences, Brittany sought work in the Washington DC area, in order to be near her fiancé who was already working at the Food and Drug Administration.

In the spring of 2014, Brittany was interviewed by CMTA CEO Patrick Livney on the recommendation of Dr. Jim Inglese. They were looking to fund a scientist to work on a drug treatment for CMT1B as part of an ongoing collaboration between the CMTA and the National Center for Advancing Translational Sciences (NCATS, a part of the National Institutes of Health) Pat and Jim were immediately impressed by Brittany's intelligence and enthusiasm and hired her on the spot. Today, Brittany is designing cellular systems, called assays, that monitor CMT1B biology and report when a chemical compound slows or stops its progression. The assays, which are tiny, are placed in small wells on a well plate, and then hundreds of thousands of chemical compounds are tested on them in an effort to find the handful of compounds that can slow or stop the disease's progression. This process has already been completed on CMT1A and a number of promising compounds have been identified.

While Brittany was brought on to develop assays for CMT1B, she also spends some of her time working with a CMT2A cell line generated by John Svaren at the University of Wisconsin. Brittany and her co-workers are currently working to validate this cell line and hope to begin the high-throughput screening of compounds soon.

Brittany says she loves working for the CMTA and finds the work extremely rewarding. She particularly enjoys working on the two very different biological pathways represented by CMT1B and CMT2A. She finds meeting members of the CMT community very motivating and plans to continue working for the CMTA as long as possible. Brittany thoroughly enjoys the highly collaborative environment at the National Center for Advancing Translational Sciences, which fosters a dynamic research environment and promotes efficient translational research.

When asked, Brittany stated that with more funding, more staff could be brought on board, the speed of her research could be increased, and additional CMT subtypes could be studied. But for now, the CMTA and the NIH have a great collaborative partnership in place, and are setting the tone for collaborative research for other diseases. Brittany is honored to be a part of CMT research.

When not working, Brittany enjoys hiking and playing with her two cats, Lewis and Clark.

Shawna Feely

The Charcot-Marie-Tooth Association has identified 20 Centers of Excellence that provide outstanding multidisciplinary medical treatment for people with CMT. One of these is the CMT Clinic at the University of Iowa. At the UI CMT Clinic, Lead Genetic Counselor Shawna Feely works closely with Director/Neurologist Dr. Mike Shy to provide exceptional patient care and to lead the world-wide research being undertaken by the Inherited Neuropathies Foundation into the causes and eventual treatments for CMT.

In her dual role as lead genetic counselor at the clinic and international research coordinator for the Inherited Neuropathies Foundation, Shawna Feely is one of the most knowledgeable resources in the world on the specific genetic causes and possible treatments for CMT. I was lucky enough to meet Shawna on a visit to Maryland, and I interviewed her to learn more about her background and the current state of CMT treatment and research.

Shawna Feely

Growing up in the Seattle area with a father who was an oceanographer and a great grandfather who was a botanist, Shawna Feely always knew she would become a scientist, she just didn't know what kind. Aware that Shawna's energetic and outgoing personality was not suited for a life spent looking into a microscope, a college advisor suggested that she become a genetic counselor, so with little knowledge of the specifics of the profession, Shawna set her course.

After a young life spent in numerous cities, including Seattle, Portland, Los Angeles, San Francisco, New York, Boston, London, and Detroit, Shawna was recruited by Dr. Mike Shy to come to The University of Iowa and build a neuro-genetics program as part of the University of Iowa Department of Neurology.

The IU Neuro-genetic clinic treats patients with a number of neurologic issues, including Huntington's Disease, muscular dystrophy, ALS, and of course, CMT. Folks suffering from neurologic disorders regularly travel from all over the globe to visit the University of Iowa clinic. Shawna's very first

89

patient in 2012 was from Australia, and in just the last few years they have welcomed folks from over 24 countries and all 50 states. Thursdays are devoted to full day multidisciplinary evaluations and treatments for patients with CMT.

While much of Shawna's time is devoted to seeing patients, she also works with and coordinates much of the research work of the Inherited Neuropathies Consortium. Shawn reports that the INC is a powerful engine for driving CMT research forward through its international network. One of the projects currently underway at INC is finding a reliable methodology for measuring the progression of CMT over time. Having this methodology in place will allow scientists to measure the effectiveness of drugs currently in development once clinical trials begin.

Shawna is also working on a study specifically looking into CMT2A. This CMT subtype often progresses rapidly in the first two decades of an individual's life, often leaving folks who have it in a wheelchair. Shawna and other scientists are looking into the specific genetic causes for this CMT behavior and the other genetic mutations that cause it.

After four years in Iowa, Shawna reports that she does not mind the Iowa winters, but was surprised by the warmth of the summers, when temperatures can climb as high as 108. She also reports that she has gained a nuanced appreciation of corn in all its many facets, although there are folks in her office from New Jersey who insist that the corn from their state is superior to Iowa's.

8
My Story

"I am not what happened to me.
I am what I choose to become."

Carl Jung

Clark Semmes

I am lucky

I am one of the lucky ones. I have a relatively mild case of CMT. I did not know anything was wrong with me until I was 55 years old. I played football in high school. I played rugby in college. One summer I rode my bicycle up the coast of California. I even tried to bicycle across the country once, but only got from Maryland to Texas. To this day I have never fallen because of an inability to lift the front of my feet. This is not the typical story.

In the profiles that I write periodically for The CMTA Report, and in listening to my CMT buddies I more often hear stories of childhood clumsiness, adolescent diagnosis, and braces, surgeries, and even wheelchairs in the 20s and 30s. These are painful, often heart-breaking stories, some of which include botched surgeries and horrific falls. The more common story is one of feeling "clumsy" from an early age. The more common story is one of numerous falls that are painful both physically and emotionally. Getting braces on your legs at an age when one is the most self-conscious, that is the typical story. For plenty of people, Charcot-Marie- Tooth disease starts much earlier and is much more debilitating.

My Story

While my diagnosis did not come until I was 55, there were warning signs that I had CMT, had anyone been watching. One of the tell-tale signs of CMT is a hammertoe. This is a toe that takes a sharp downward turn at the knuckle. Why does CMT cause hammertoe? CMT is a disease of the peripheral nerves, the ones that tell your legs and your arms what to do, slowly deteriorating. The longest peripheral nerve is the one from your brain to your toes, so your toes are the first thing to be affected. When the nerves die, the muscles soon follow and when you lose the muscles in your toes they begin to bend into a hammertoe.

Both my big toes have been hammered for as long as I can remember. I can clearly remember injuring my feet at the age of 8 or 9 and having a gaggle of kids gather around to study my injury. I remember everyone agreeing my big toes were clearly broken based on their crazy appearance. Had anyone been watching, this would have been an early indication of CMT.

There was also my father. CMT is a genetic disease. It is usually (but not always) inherited. My father had the skinniest legs I have ever seen. Being generally lighthearted and always handy with a joke, my father had a number of lines he would use when someone commented on his legs.

If someone said, "What happened to your legs?" his first response would be, "I don't know, they were swollen up like this when I woke up this morning?"

He would also tell people he was considering suing his legs for "non-support."

Now that my father has passed away, and I have been diagnosed, it is clear to me that the cause of my father's skinny legs was CMT. I now recall him also speaking of neuropathy in his feet, which for me confirms the diagnosis. If I needed more evidence, I needed only recall the way that his hands trembled, another symptom of this disease. Had I really been watching, my father's ailments would have alerted me to my own situation.

Amazingly, although I am almost certain my father had CMT, he never used any kind of support to walk, and only fell once, of which I am aware, when he fell and broke his hip at the age of 86. From the day of that fall, my father fell into a spiral of ever-worsening health that would end in his death almost exactly one year later. That year was an incredibly hectic time for me as I bounced between my job and his bedside.

During this time I began to notice that my feet were numb a great deal of the time and that I was having difficulty typing. At first, I assumed that my feet were numb because of the shoes I was wearing and that my hands were shaking as a result of too much caffeine, but as my father moved ever closer to his eventual death, it slowly dawned on me that something was not right.

Once my dad passed away, and his affairs and everyone's emotions settled, I finally had a little time to pursue the issue of my numb feet. As I reflected on it, I recalled an annual physical and a test where my doctor would touch my feet with a pin and ask for me to signal when I felt the pin. I always failed this test. I can remember locking eyes with my doctor as he waited for me to signal that I felt the pin in each new location. I also remember me waiting anxiously for the touch of the pin but never getting the signal. The fact that I consistently failed this test was never something that my doctor mentioned or acted on, but now as I attempted to discern why my feet were always numb, it seemed important.

The first few doctors I went to examined my feet carefully, but gave no opinion as to why they were numb. I clearly remember one telling me it "might be a touch of neuropathy," a phrase that stuck in my craw at the time.

Numbness and lack of feeling are pretty much the definition of neuropathy. Clearly it was neuropathy, the question was why was there neuropathy?

Out of patience and lacking any answers, I finally decided that if the problem was in my feet, I should see a podiatrist. This turned out to be a lucky decision. Dr. Jose DeBorja of Easton, Maryland, took off my shoes and socks on my first visit and immediately began making observations about my feet.

"You have hammertoes," he stated.

"You have high arches," he continued.

When I told him about my neuropathy, he quickly gave me his diagnosis.

"I think you have a degenerative nerve disease called Charcot-Marie-Tooth."

Like most people, I had never heard of this disease and the first thing I asked was if he would write it down on a piece of paper.

Turning Point

When I was first diagnosed I fell into a depression. Not a small depression. It was a big depression. It was the kind of depression that an asteroid makes when it hits the moon. It was an everything-is-dark, not-get-out-of-bed-for-days kind of depression. I remember it lasting a month. My wife remembers it lasting longer. I guess depressions are like that. They are hard on the depressed, but they are even harder on those who love the person who is depressed.

I think depression often come from a sense of loss. When one is diagnosed, one only focuses on what has been lost. People with CMT imagine losing some or many of their physical abilities. It is undeniable. People with CMT cannot do everything that folks without it can do. But I think what people miss is how much people with disabilities can do. I began my climb out of depression by reading a biography of Franklin Roosevelt. Franklin Roosevelt guided the United States through the Great Depression and World War II while completely paralyzed from the waist down. Talk about braces – that man had some braces! Next I read a biography of Stephen Hawking. Stephen Hawking barely has use of his body, yet is a best-selling author and one of the world's greatest physicists. Who was I to complain?

One day soon after my diagnosis, I was in a small dog park in my hometown of Oxford, Maryland when I noticed a woman with a slightly odd gait (at the time, I was obsessed with peoples gaits). For whatever reason, I approached her and said something about noticing the odd way she walked. I told her I was interested in people's gaits because I had recently been diagnosed with Charcot–Marie–... To my utter amazement, she filled in the last word... Tooth. She had the same disease! Her name was Penny Naylor, and we talked for quite a while. She was the first person I met who also had CMT! She was neither depressed nor unhappy. It was a revelation at the time. She directed me to a person in a nearby town whom she described as a "CMT activist." Her name was Missy Warfield. She suggested I call her.

Missy Warfield turned out to be the Easton Branch Leader of the CMTA. When I called her, she graciously invited my wife and me to her home. Missy was the opposite of depressed. She was kind and understanding and encouraging. Over iced tea and cookies on Missy's back porch, she explained to me that she had inherited CMT1A from her mother, and unwittingly passed it on to her son and now her grand-children. A devoted CMT activist, Missy had raised many hundreds of thousands dollars for the CMTA, and devoted much of her life to finding a cure. The darkness that had clouded my thoughts began to dissipate on the day that I met Missy.

A few weeks later, a friend gave me the phone number of another CMT activist who lived in Baltimore and every year swam across the Chesapeake Bay to raise money for the CMTA. I had to meet this guy. I gave him a call, and was once again graciously invited to someone's home. His name was Steve O'Donnell. Far from being depressed, Steve is a guy who is fully alive 100 percent of the time. Despite a fairly serious case of CMT, Steve is an amazing athlete, a highly successful businessman, and a guy who eats life for breakfast, lunch, and dinner. His gusto for life is off the scale. I am now proud to call him one of my closest friends. He is a living testament to how much one can accomplish despite a disability like CMT. The day I met Steve was the day I put down my remaining depression and became a CMT activist.

CMT Activist

I started by going to a CMTA Conference in Florida. There I met Jeana Sweeny, Elizabeth Ouellette, Patrick Livney, Steve Weiss, and others who have dedicated much of their lives to putting an end to CMT. It is hard to describe the warmth and generosity of spirit with which I was welcomed to this new family. Sitting in a large conference room filled with people suffering from the same curious affliction as myself, I suddenly felt less alone, less isolated. I was not just one person, or even part of a small group. I was now a member of a tribe!

Returning home, I was determined to do whatever I could to support the CMTA. My first act was to volunteer to be a Branch Leader. For anyone who is considering becoming a branch leader, I wholeheartedly recommend it. The CMTA has everything you will need to get started. They have preprinted announcements, they have e-mail lists of folks in your area with CMT, and they have complete instructions on what to do. There are still things that the branch leaders themselves must do, including finding speakers, but I found the entire process to be amazingly gratifying and fulfilling. I have now been the leader of the Baltimore branch of the CMTA for about two years. And I have met more wonderful people than I can count and made lots of new friends. I would not trade the experience for anything in the world.

My next step was to hold a fundraiser. This is not something I had any experience with, but I pushed forward nonetheless. It was winter, so an outdoor event seemed out of the question. Fortunately there was a popular little restaurant in Oxford just a few blocks from my house. With nothing to lose, I approached the owner, and asked if she would consider hosting a fundraiser for the CMTA. She agreed, we picked the date, and we were off and running. I invited everyone I knew. The event turned out to be a great success. My new friends Missy and Steve both attended, the three of us gave little speeches, and we raised about $2,000 for the CMTA.

When I sent in the proceeds of our fundraiser, Jeana Sweeney asked me if I would write up the event for the CMTA newsletter. I think winter is a slow time for fundraisers, so perhaps they needed the copy. I dutifully wrote a few short paragraphs and to my great surprise, it made it into the newsletter. One of the things I included in the article was a brief mention of some more fundraising ideas we had brainstormed during the party. One was an online Words-with-Friends tournament. I wasn't even really sure what this meant, but I had needed a way to end a paragraph so I stuck it in.

When CMTA Board Vice Chair Elizabeth Ouellette read my article, I guess the Words-with-Friends suggestion rang a bell. She e-mailed me and mentioned that she had also been considering a Words with Friends tournament as a form of fundraising. The next step seemed clear. To make a long story short, I think we have now had four CMTA Words with Friends tournaments. Folks seem to enjoy them and each one raises about $1,000 for the CMTA.

That spring, my new friend, Steve O'Donnell, mentioned to me that he was having some trouble with his annual swim across the Chesapeake Bay. The organizers of the bay swim didn't like the fact that he was raising funds for his charity (the CMTA) during their event, which was raising money for another charity. I told Steve there was an annual one-mile swim in my tiny hometown of Oxford, Maryland and that he was welcome to join and raise money for any charity he wanted. Steve liked this idea, but did not think that just a swim was a sufficient enough challenge, so we decided to tack on a 20 mile bike ride (I am not a swimmer, but I could do the bike ride). We decided to name the event the Oxford Biathlon. While I am a feather weight in the field of fund-raising, Steve is a heavy hitter and even though we threw it together at the last minute, the event was a total success, raising more than $100,000 for the CMTA. The event is now an annual occurrence and gets bigger every year.

Almost a year ago, I heard that beloved staff member and longtime editor of The CMTA Report, Pat Dreibelbis, suddenly passed away. Without giving it much thought, I volunteered my wife Marica, a life-long reporter and editor as a temporary fill-in until a permanent replacement was found. Marcia took to the job immediately and was soon given the job of Director of Print Communications for the CMTA. She loves both the work and the opportunity to work for the greater good, and I am so proud of her that there are times when I could almost bust.

So today, Marcia and I are a tiny outpost of CMT activism out here on Maryland's Eastern Shore. We both love what we do, and thrive on the sense of well-being we receive from working with the CMTA.

9

Fundraising & Secret Weapons

Fundraising

My friend, Steve O'Donnell, says that you fundraise the way that you build a house, one brick at a time. Fundraising should be a win-win. If you provide people with something that they want (an event, an experience) they will be more than happy to make a contribution.

In my humble opinion, fundraising is fun. It's like having a party. You dream up an event, you organize it, you invite all your friends and hopefully you raise a lot of money and everyone has a good time. The event itself can be anything. Pat Livney has a golf tournament, Jeana Sweeney has a softball tournament. There are swimming events, bowling events, walking events, and biking events. Steve O'Donnell used to have a swimming event, then he and I teamed up and we added a biking event. Then Missy Warfield joined us and we added a walking event and a silent auction. A fundraising event can be anything. I think anyone who has CMT should consider fundraising. No one is more motivated to cure this disease than us. We cannot wait for someone to come rescue us. It will not happen. It is up to us to seize the reins and determine our own destiny. For well over 100 years, since this disease was first discovered in the 1880s, those who had this disease had no choice but to suffer through it. There was no hope of a drug or a treatment. But today the situation is different, today the science exists to find a real treatment. As I write this, drug compounds have been identified that stop the destruction that CMT does to our nerves. Human trials will be starting in the not too distant future. There is even serious work being done on re-mylination, the repairing of damaged nerves, the reversal of CMT!

One of the first keys to fundraising is to keep a good list of all your friends, co-workers, family members, and acquaintances. These are the people you will be inviting to your event! Their contributions are the bricks from which you will build your house. A good fundraiser should keep an up-to-date list of everyone he or she knows that contains their physical address, their phone number, and their e-mail, at the least.

Secret Weapons

While I write a lot about those of us who suffer from CMT, and the many trials and challenges that we face, I can never say enough about the spouses, parents, siblings and others who do all the tiny and enormous tasks that we cannot. So I want to take this space to offer my sincerest and most heartfelt appreciation for everyone who provides assistance to someone with CMT. We appreciate every jar you open because we can't. We appreciate every button you fasten, we appreciate every sock you put on, every shoelace you tie, every place that you drive us, and every comforting word offered. We also appreciate the way you recognize when we have hit our limit and are overcome with exhaustion and muscle fatigue. We thank you for all you do!

My friend Iris Anderson calls her husband her secret weapon in her battle with CMT, because of all the myriad ways in which he helps her in her struggle. My secret weapon in the battle against CMT is my wife Marcia. From the day I was diagnosed Marcia has been a constant voice of encouragement and support. She has never given me anything but love and sympathy in response to my struggles. She probably knows more about CMT then I do, and she learns more every day. To me, Pat Livney is the four-star general in the war on CMT, and I am just a foot soldier. But Marcia is now on the staff of the CMTA and in my mind is at least a Major.

ABOUT THE AUTHOR

Clark Semmes lives in Trappe, Maryland with his wife, Marcia, and their two pugs, Wallis and Bailey. When not writing about CMT, Clark likes to tend his oyster garden.

43269098R00060

Made in the USA
San Bernardino, CA
17 December 2016